Examberry

Non-Verbal Reasoning Test 2

Multiple Choice

Read the following instructions carefully:

- Do not turn over the test paper until you are told to do so.
- All questions should be answered on your multiple choice answer sheet. Using a pencil, make a clear horizontal line through the empty box next to the correct answer.
- If you need to change an answer, rub out the incorrect answer and fill in the correct answer.
- Do not make any other marks on the answer sheet – you may write on the question paper if you find it helpful.
- You have 50 minutes to complete the test.
- Calculators and dictionaries are not allowed.

Copyright (C) Examberry Media Ltd 2019.
The right of Examberry Media Ltd to be identified as the author of this work has been asserted in accordance with the Copyright, Designs and Patents Act 1988.
All rights reserved, including translation. No part of this publication may be reproduced or transmitted in any form or by any means, electronic or mechanical, including photocopying, recording or duplication in any information storage and retrieval system, without permission in writing from the publishers, and may not be otherwise reproduced within the terms of any licence by the Copyright Licensing Agency Ltd.
Any person who commits any unauthorised act in relation to this publication may be liable to criminal prosecution and civil claims or damages.
First published in 2019 by Examberry Media Ltd, International House, 142 Cromwell Road, Kensington, London SW7 4EF.

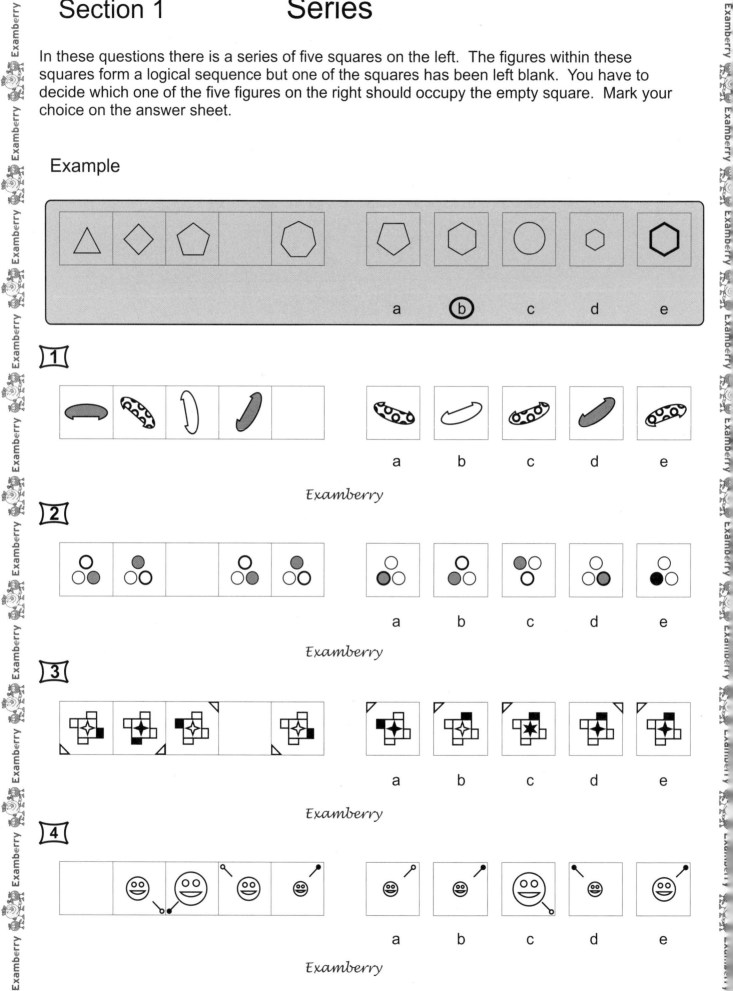

Section 1 Page 2

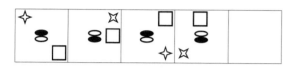 

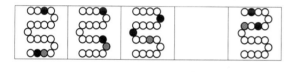 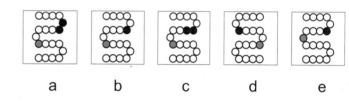

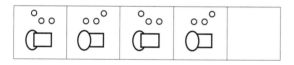 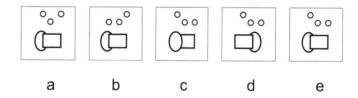

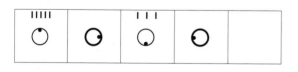 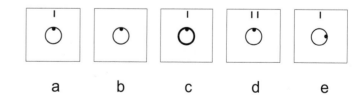

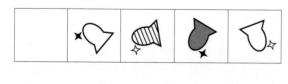 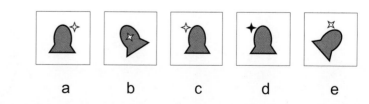

Section 1 Page 3

11

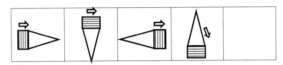

a b c d e

12

a b c d e

13

a b c d e

14

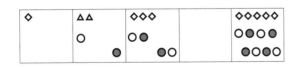

a b c d e

15

a b c d e

16

a b c d e

Section 2 : Codes

In these questions there are four or five figures on the left together with code letters which represent features of these figures. There is a further figure which does not have code letters associated with it. You have to decide which one of the five possible codes on the right should represent this figure. Mark your choice on the answer sheet.

Example

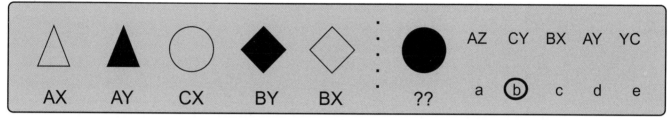

1

2

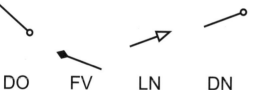 

3

4

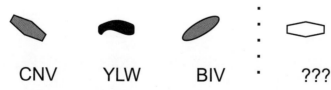

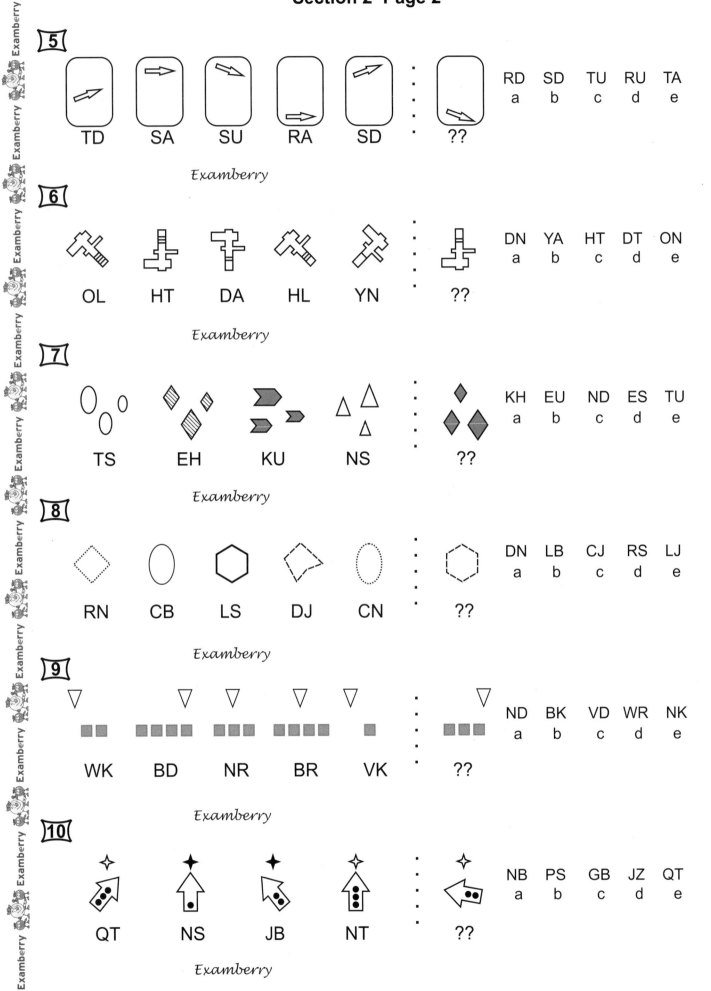

Section 2 Page 3

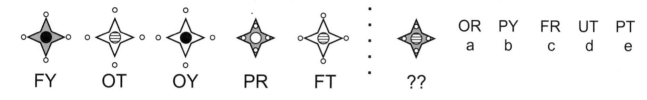
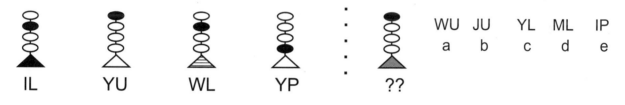
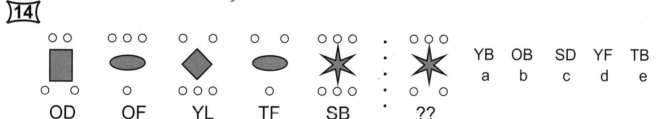

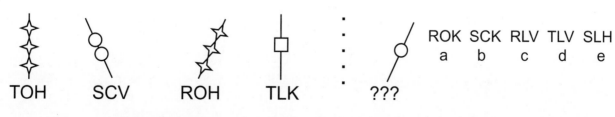

Section 3   Analogies

In these questions there are two figures on the left separated by an arrow. You have to decide how these two figures are related. There is a third figure which is separated by an arrow from five further figures on the right. You have to decide which one of these five figures is related to the third figure in the same way as the first two figures are related to each other. Mark your choice on the answer sheet.

Example

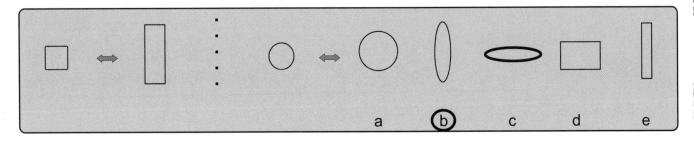

1

 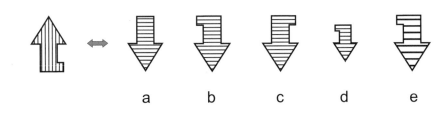

2

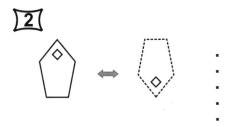 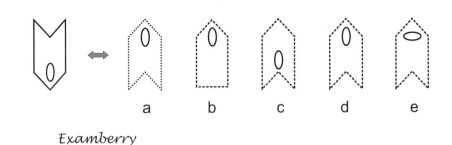

3

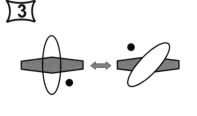 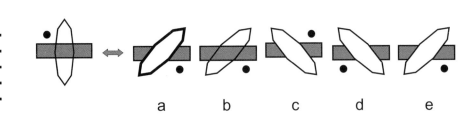

4

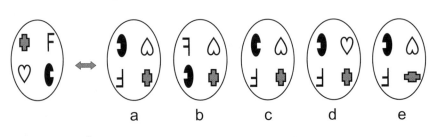

Section 3 Page 2

5 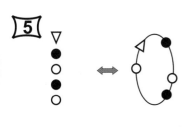 :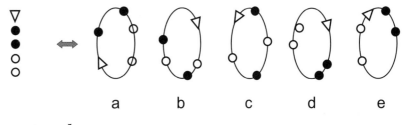

a b c d e

6 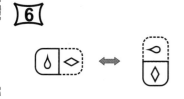 :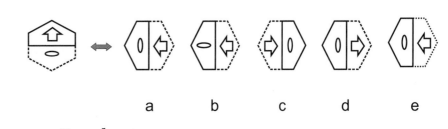

a b c d e

7 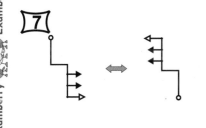 :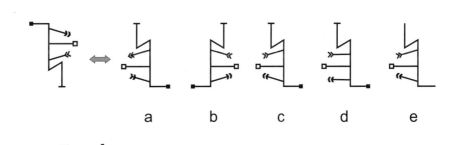

a b c d e

8 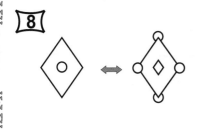 :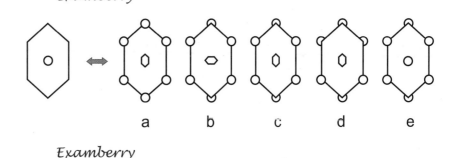

a b c d e

9 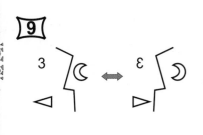 :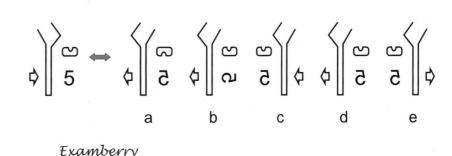

a b c d e

10 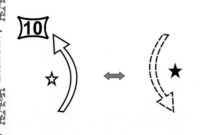 :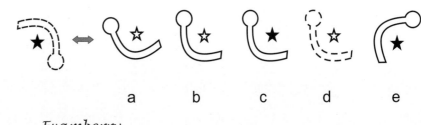

a b c d e

Section 3 Page 3

11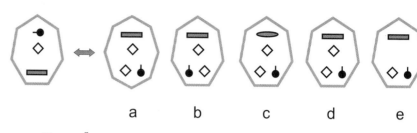

a b c d e

12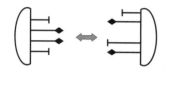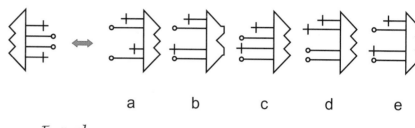

a b c d e

13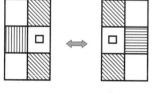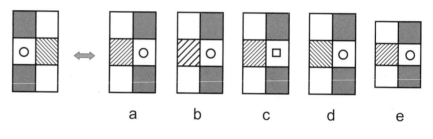

a b c d e

14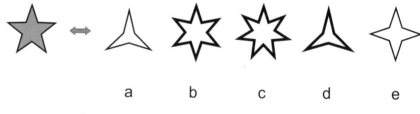

a b c d e

15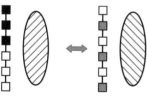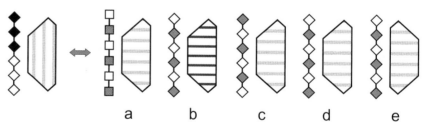

a b c d e

16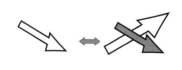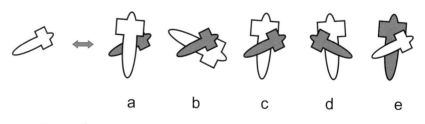

a b c d e

Section 4 — Matrix

In these questions there is a grid on the left with 4 or 9 squares one of which has been left blank. Look at the figures on the right and decide which one would best complete the pattern in the grid. Mark your choice on the answer sheet.

Example

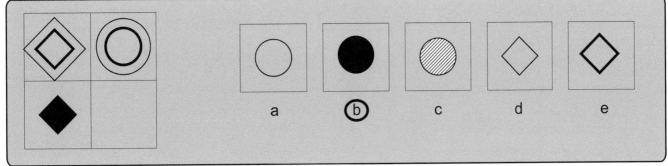

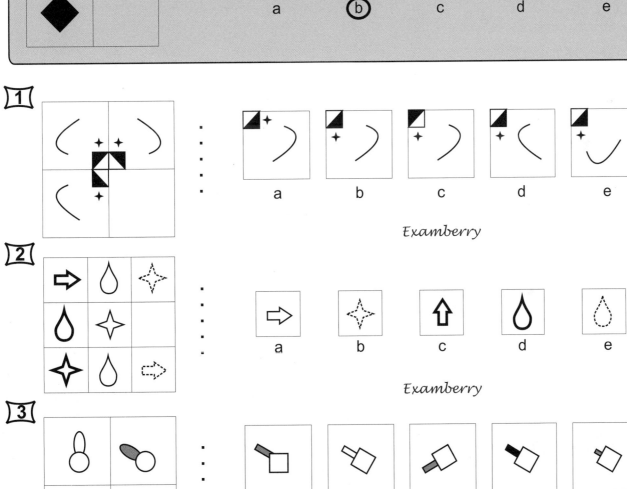

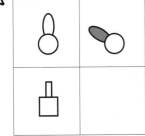

a b c d e

Examberry

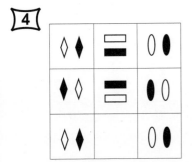

a b c d e

Examberry

Section 4 Page 2

5 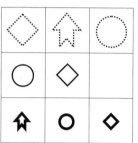 :
   a b c d e

6 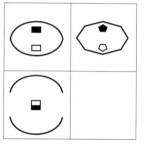 :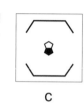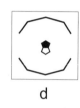
   a b c d e

7 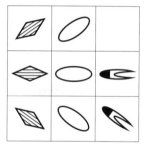 :
   a b c d e

8 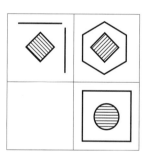 :
   a b c d e

9 :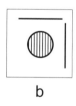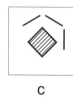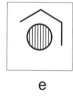
   a b c d e

10 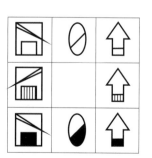 :
   a b c d e

Section 4 Page 3

11.
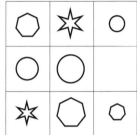 :
    a   b   c   d   e

12.
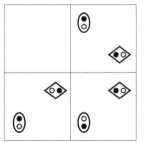 :
    a   b   c   d   e

13.
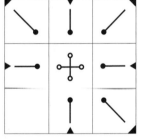 :
    a   b   c   d   e

14.
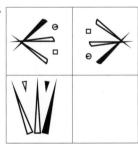 :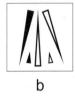
    a   b   c   d   e

15.
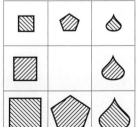 :
    a   b   c   d   e

16.
 :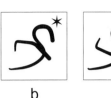
    a   b   c   d   e

Section 5 Odd One Out

In these questions there are five figures, four of which have something in common. You have to decide which one of the five is the 'odd one out'. Mark your choice on the answer sheet.

Example

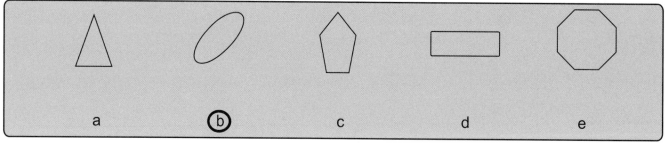

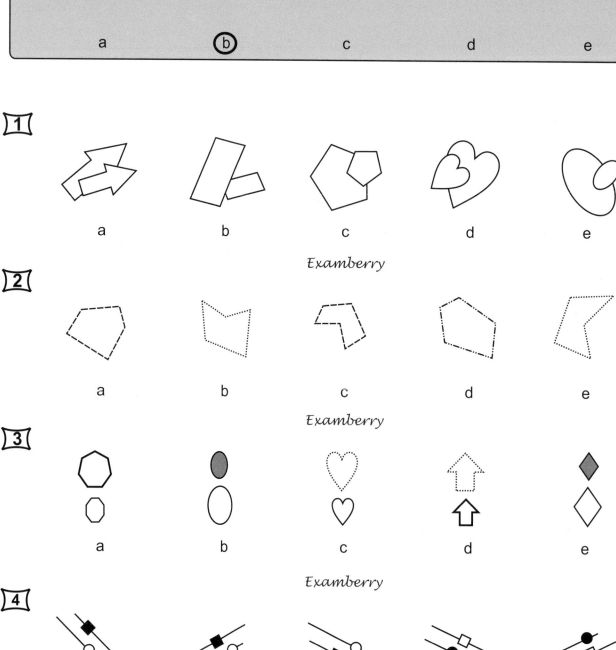

Section 5 Page 2

a   b   c   d   e

    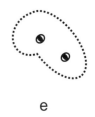

a   b   c   d   e

 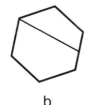  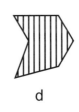 

a   b   c   d   e

   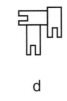

a   b   c   d   e

a   b   c   d   e

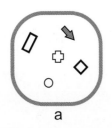 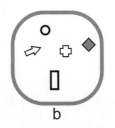  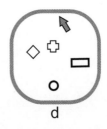 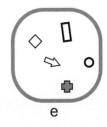

a   b   c   d   e

Section 5 Page 3

11

a b c d e

12

a b c d e

13

a b c d e

14

a b c d e

15

a b c d e

16

a b c d e

End of Test

Examberry

Non-Verbal Reasoning Test 3

Multiple Choice

Read the following instructions carefully:

- Do not turn over the test paper until you are told to do so.
- All questions should be answered on your multiple choice answer sheet. Using a pencil, make a clear horizontal line through the empty box next to the correct answer.
- If you need to change an answer, rub out the incorrect answer and fill in the correct answer.
- Do not make any other marks on the answer sheet – you may write on the question paper if you find it helpful.
- You have 50 minutes to complete the test.
- Calculators and dictionaries are not allowed.

Copyright (C) Examberry Media Ltd 2019.
The right of Examberry Media Ltd to be identified as the author of this work has been asserted in accordance with the Copyright, Designs and Patents Act 1988.
All rights reserved, including translation. No part of this publication may be reproduced or transmitted in any form or by any means, electronic or mechanical, including photocopying, recording or duplication in any information storage and retrieval system, without permission in writing from the publishers, and may not be photocopied or otherwise reproduced within the terms of any licence by the Copyright Licensing Agency Ltd.
Any person who commits any unauthorised act in relation to this publication may be liable to criminal prosecution and civil claims or damages.
First published in 2019 by Examberry Media Ltd, International House, 142 Cromwell Road, Kensington, London SW7 4EF.

Section 1 Analogies

In these questions there are two figures on the left separated by an arrow. You have to decide how these two figures are related. There is a third figure which is separated by an arrow from five further figures on the right. You have to decide which one of these five figures is related to the third figure in the same way as the first two figures are related to each other. Mark your choice on the answer sheet.

Example

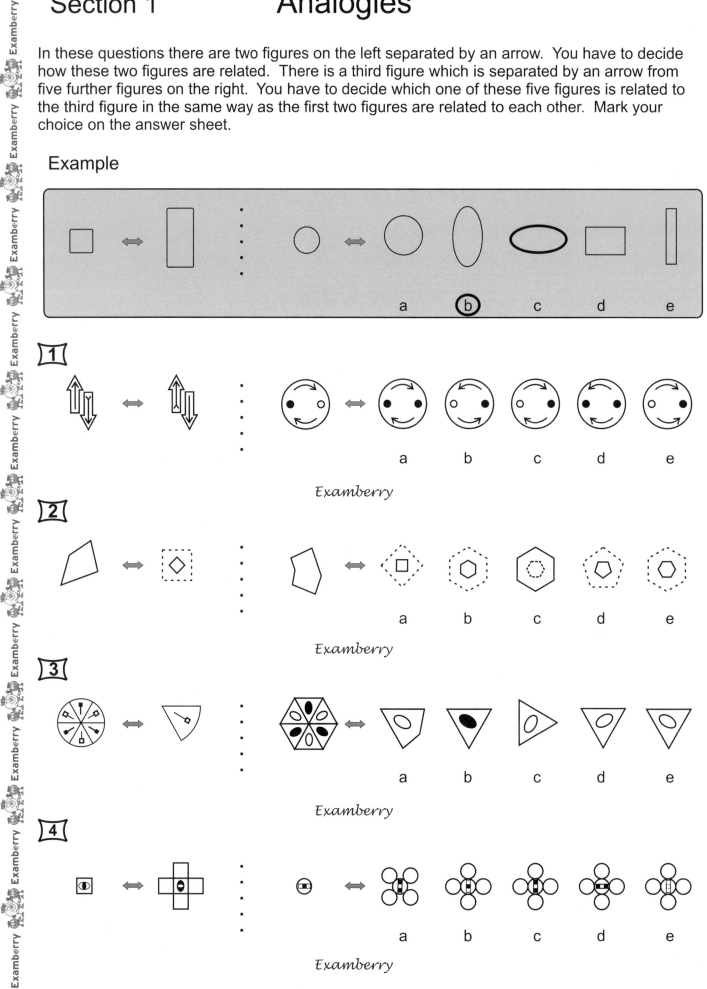

Section 1 Page 2

5

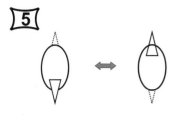 :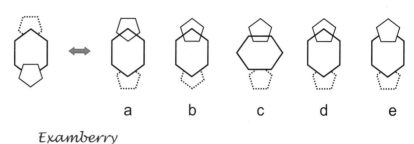

a   b   c   d   e

Examberry

6

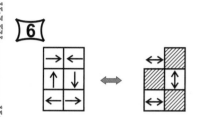 :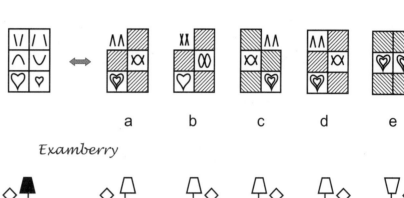

a   b   c   d   e

Examberry

7

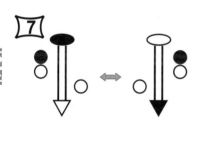 :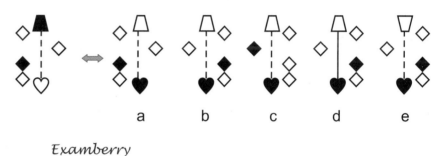

a   b   c   d   e

Examberry

8

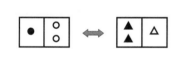 :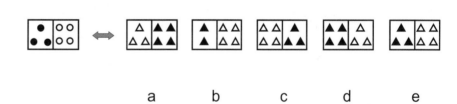

a   b   c   d   e

Examberry

9

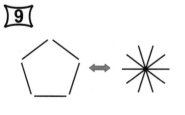 :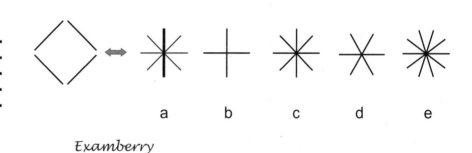

a   b   c   d   e

Examberry

10

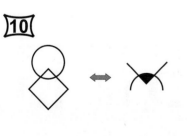 :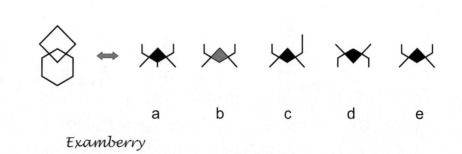

a   b   c   d   e

Examberry

Section 1 Page 3

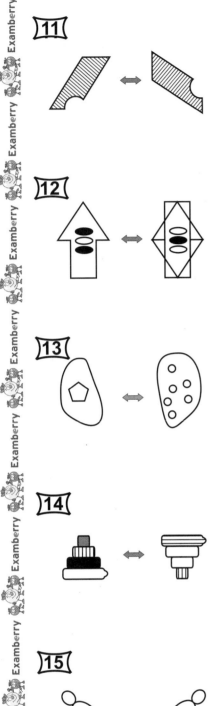
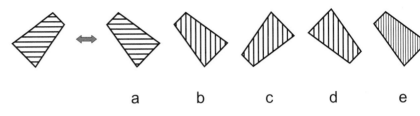

a b c d e

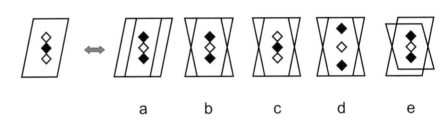

a b c d e

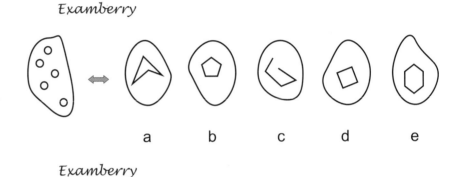

a b c d e

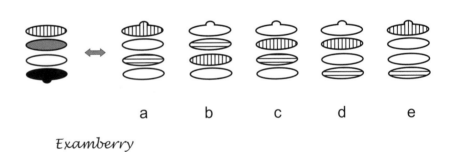

a b c d e

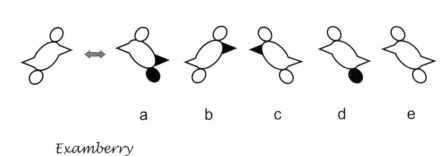

a b c d e

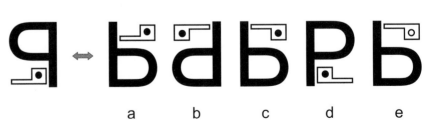

a b c d e

Section 2 Series

In these questions there is a series of five squares on the left. The figures within these squares form a logical sequence but one of the squares has been left blank. You have to decide which one of the five figures on the right should occupy the empty square. Mark your choice on the answer sheet.

Example

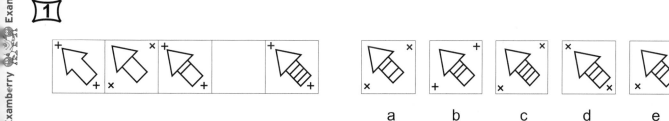

1
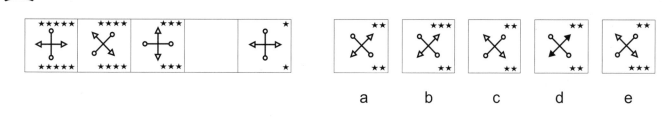

2

3
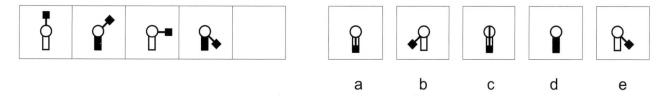

4
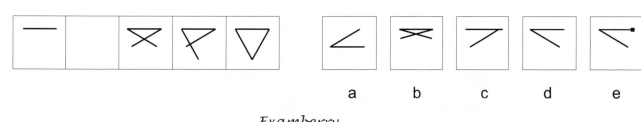

Section 2 Page 2

5

a b c d e

6

a b c d e

7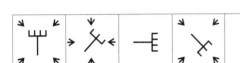

a b c d e

8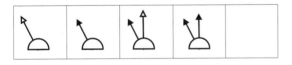

a b c d e

9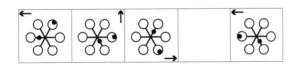

a b c d e

10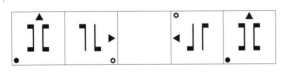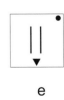

a b c d e

Section 2 Page 3

11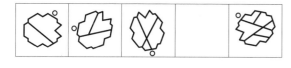

   a   b   c   d   e

12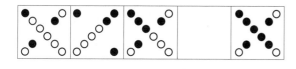

   a   b   c   d   e

13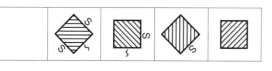

   a   b   c   d   e

14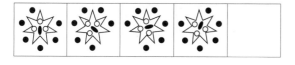

   a   b   c   d   e

15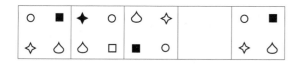

   a   b   c   d   e

16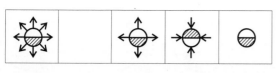

   a   b   c   d   e

Section 3   Belongs With

In these questions the two figures on the left have something in common. You have to decide which one of the five shapes on the right 'belongs with' the two on the left. Mark your choice on the answer sheet.

Example

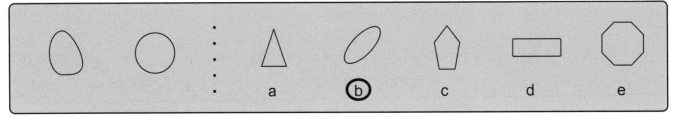

1

  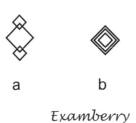 

                               a   b   c   d   e

Examberry

2

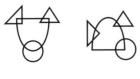

                               a   b   c   d   e

Examberry

3

                               a   b   c   d   e

Examberry

4

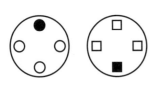     

                               a   b   c   d   e

Examberry

Section 3 Page 2

5   :
    a   b   c   d   e

6   :
    a   b   c   d   e

7   :
    a   b   c   d   e

8   :
    a   b   c   d   e

9   :
    a   b   c   d   e

10   :
    a   b   c   d   e

Section 3 Page 3

11   :

a b c d e

12   :

a b c d e

13   :

a b c d e

14   :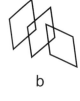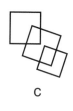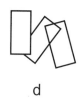

a b c d e

15   :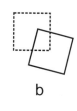

a b c d e

16   :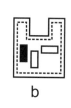

a b c d e

Section 4 Codes

In these questions there are four or five figures on the left together with code letters which represent features of these figures. There is a further figure which does not have code letters associated with it. You have to decide which one of the five possible codes on the right should represent this figure. Mark your choice on the answer sheet.

Example

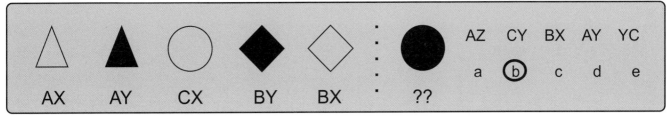

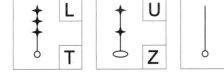 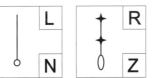 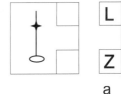 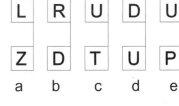

     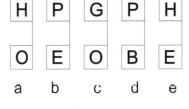

     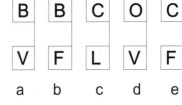

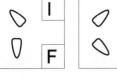   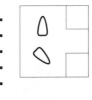 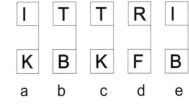

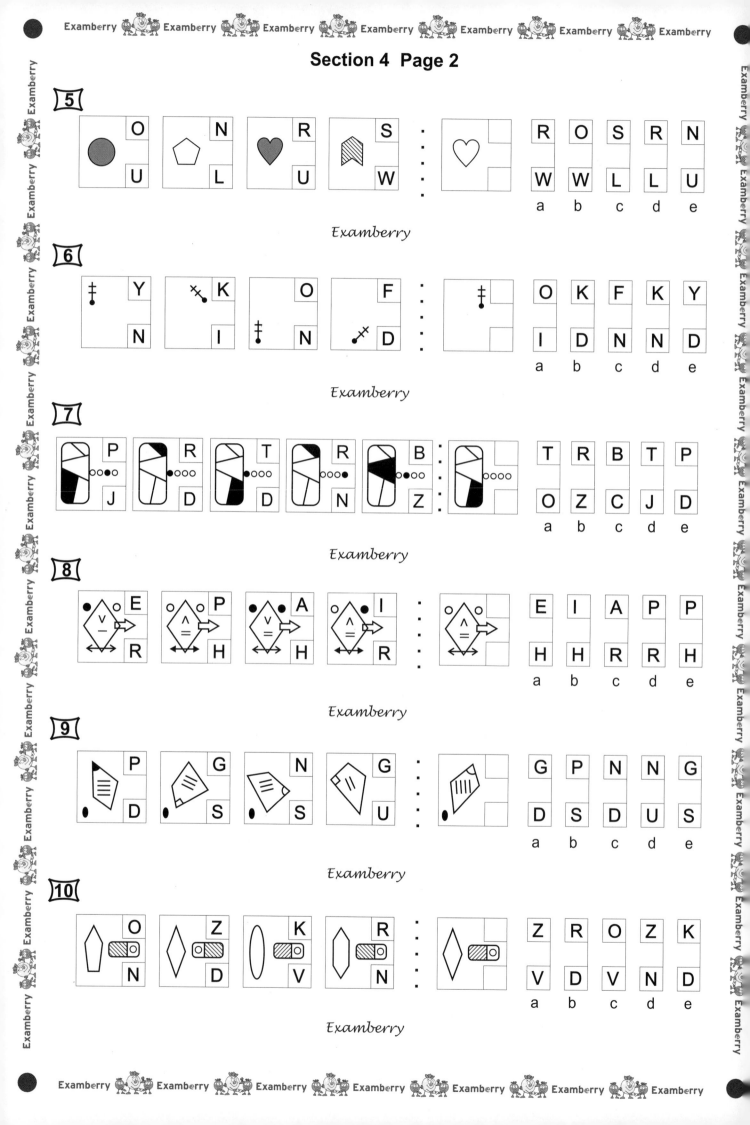

Section 4 Page 3

    :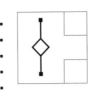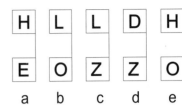

    :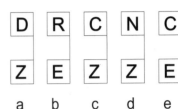

    :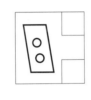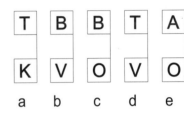

    :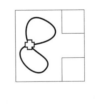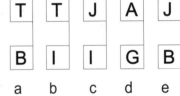

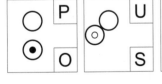   :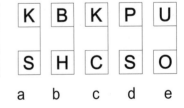

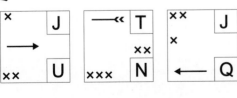 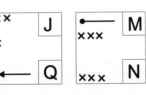 :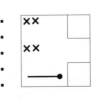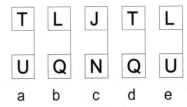

Section 5   Matrix

In these questions there is a grid on the left with 4 or 9 squares one of which has been left blank. Look at the figures on the right and decide which one would best complete the pattern in the grid. Mark your choice on the answer sheet.

Example

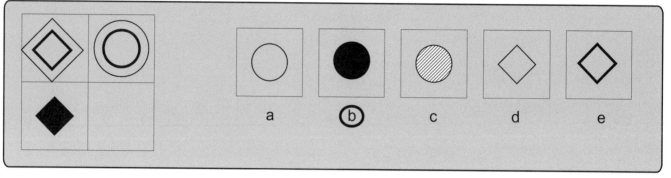

1

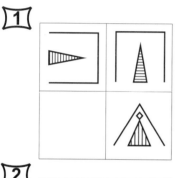
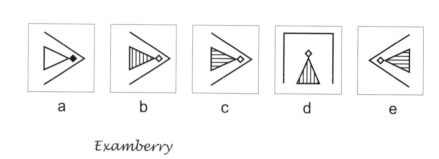

Examberry

2

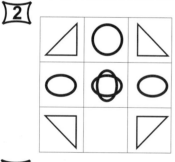
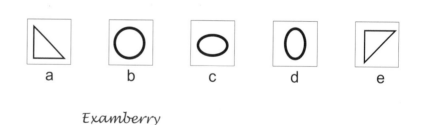

Examberry

3

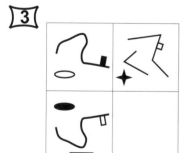
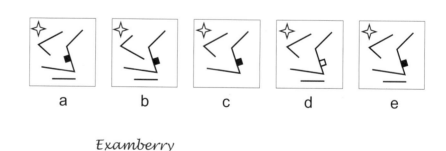

Examberry

4

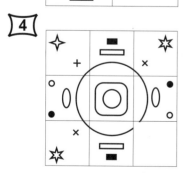
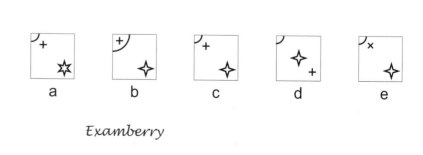

Examberry

5

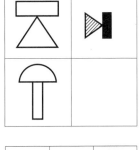

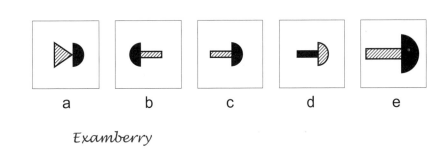

a b c d e

6

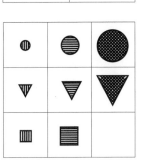

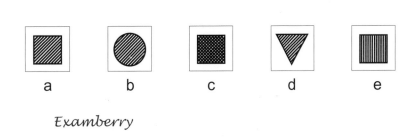

a b c d e

7

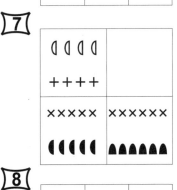

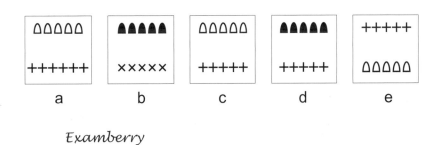

a b c d e

8

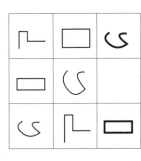

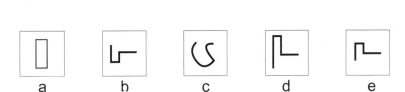

a b c d e

9

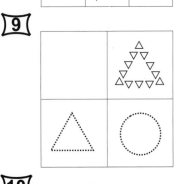

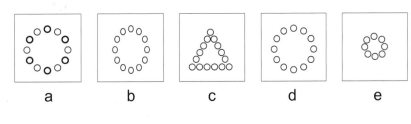

a b c d e

10

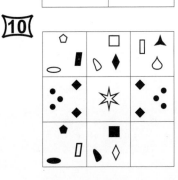

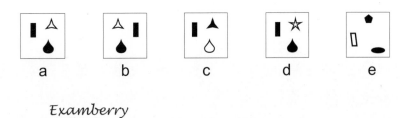

a b c d e

Section 5 Page 3

11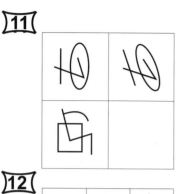

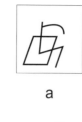   
a · b · c · d · e

Examberry

12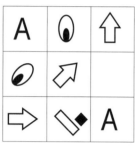

a · b · c · d · e

Examberry

13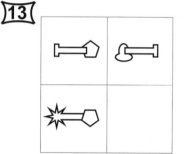

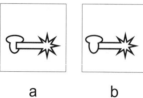 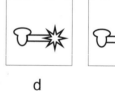
a · b · c · d · e

Examberry

14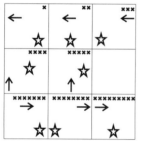

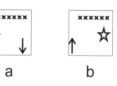
a · b · c · d · e

Examberry

15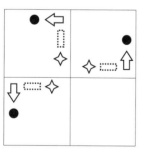

   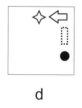 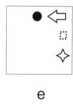
a · b · c · d · e

Examberry

16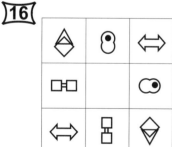

a · b · c · d · e

Examberry

End of Test

Examberry

Non-Verbal Reasoning Test 4

Multiple Choice

Read the following instructions carefully:

- Do not turn over the test paper until you are told to do so.
- All questions should be answered on your multiple choice answer sheet. Using a pencil, make a clear horizontal line through the empty box next to the correct answer.
- If you need to change an answer, rub out the incorrect answer and fill in the correct answer.
- Do not make any other marks on the answer sheet – you may write on the question paper if you find it helpful.
- You have 50 minutes to complete the test.
- Calculators and dictionaries are not allowed.

Copyright (C) Examberry Media Ltd 2019.
The right of Examberry Media Ltd to be identified as the author of this work has been asserted in accordance with the Copyright, Designs and Patents Act 1988.
All rights reserved, including translation. No part of this publication may be reproduced or transmitted in any form or by any means, electronic or mechanical, including photocopying, recording or duplication in any information storage and retrieval system, without permission in writing from the publishers, and may not be photocopied or otherwise reproduced within the terms of any licence by the Copyright Licensing Agency Ltd. Any person who commits any unauthorised act in relation to this publication may be liable to criminal prosecution and civil claims or damages.
First published in 2019 by Examberry Media Ltd, International House, 142 Cromwell Road, Kensington, London SW7 4EF.

Section 1   Matrix

In these questions there is a grid on the left with 4 or 9 squares one of which has been left blank. Look at the figures on the right and decide which one would best complete the pattern in the grid. Mark your choice on the answer sheet.

Example

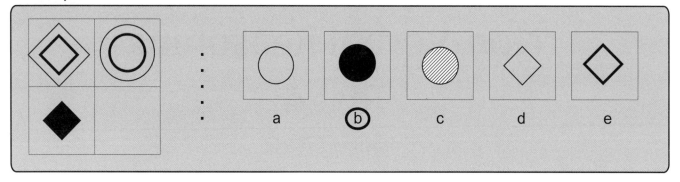

1.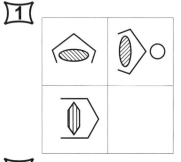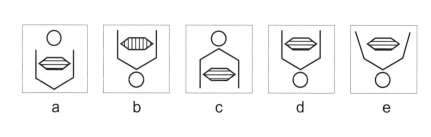

2.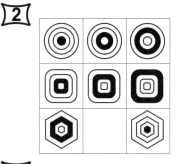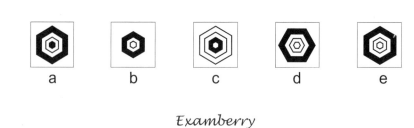

3.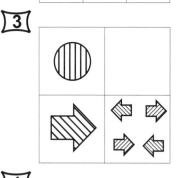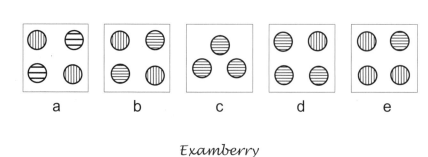

4.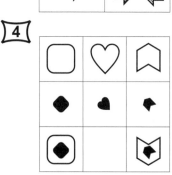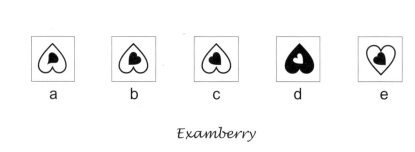

Section 1 Page 2

5 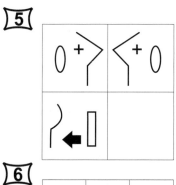 :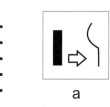

a b c d e

Examberry

6 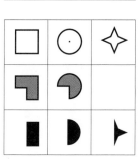 :

a b c d e

Examberry

7 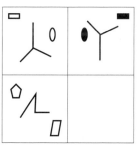 :

a b c d e

Examberry

8 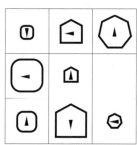 :

a b c d e

Examberry

9 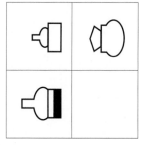 :

a b c d e

Examberry

10 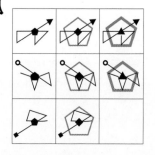 :

a b c d e

Examberry

Section 1 Page 3

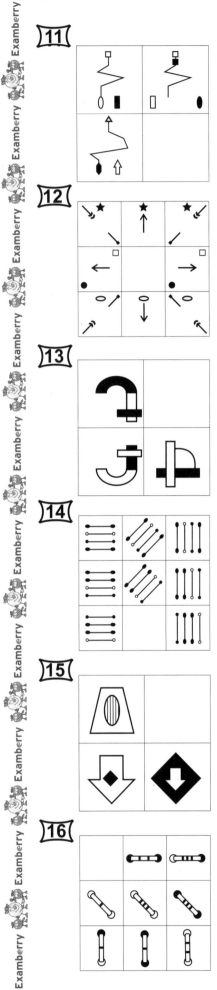

11)
 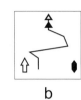 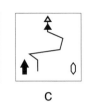 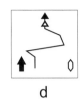 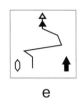
a　　b　　c　　d　　e

12)

a　　b　　c　　d　　e

13)

a　　b　　c　　d　　e

14)

a　　b　　c　　d　　e

15)
    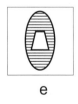
a　　b　　c　　d　　e

16)

a　　b　　c　　d　　e

Section 2 — Codes

In these questions there are four or five figures on the left together with code letters which represent features of these figures. There is a further figure which does not have code letters associated with it. You have to decide which one of the five possible codes on the right should represent this figure. Mark your choice on the answer sheet.

Example

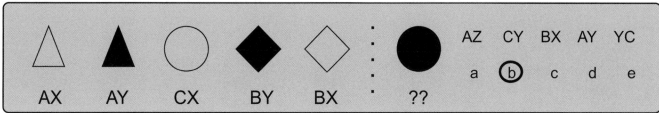

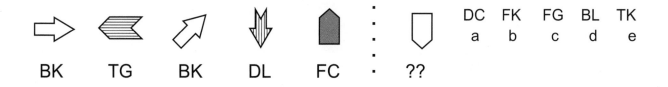

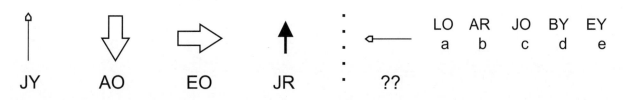

Section 2 Page 2

5

UI FD FL KD FN : ??

FN	UL	KL	UD	KI
a	b	c	d	e

6

PY WJ GX KY GZ : ??

WX	GJ	PZ	KJ	GY
a	b	c	d	e

7

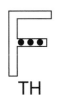  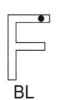 

TH BV BL CH : ??

TL	CL	BH	CV	TV
a	b	c	d	e

8

YA OU BQ NQ OP : ??

NA	NU	OQ	BP	BA
a	b	c	d	e

9

RM CK DI UM CF : ??

CI	RK	UI	UF	DM
a	b	c	d	e

10

   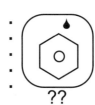

VJ TU TD SU : ??

SJ	TD	VU	SU	TJ
a	b	c	d	e

Section 2 Page 3

11

PHC TUA SZC MZB TKB

	MKB	SUB	THA	PZC	SHA
	a	b	c	d	e

???

12

HJ   FT   UT   DO   HP   :   DJ

OP   DE   DN   CB   KP   ??

DB	CP	OB	ON	KE
a	b	c	d	e

13

YU JD PU JK

??

PK	YD	JU	PD	YK
a	b	c	d	e

14

RS DT EV NT NH

??

ET	DS	NV	RH	DV
a	b	c	d	e

15

CJ HN UL BS UN

??

UJ	HS	CS	BN	CL
a	b	c	d	e

16

OH TE MF TZ

??

OF	MZ	MH	OE	TF
a	b	c	d	e

Section 3 — Belongs With

In these questions the two figures on the left have something in common. You have to decide which one of the five shapes on the right 'belongs with' the two on the left. Mark your choice on the answer sheet.

Example

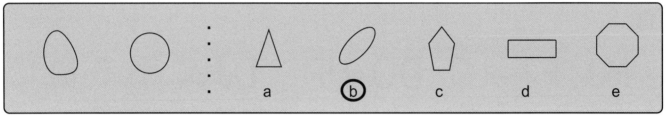

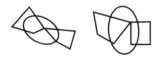

a   b   c   d   e

a   b   c   d   e

a   b   c   d   e

a   b   c   d   e

Section 3 Page 2

5   :
   a   b   c   d   e

6   :
   a   b   c   d   e

7   :
   a   b   c   d   e

8   :
   a   b   c   d   e

9   :
   a   b   c   d   e

10   :
   a   b   c   d   e

Section 3 Page 3

11   :

a b c d e

12   :

a b c d e

13 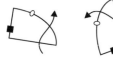 :

a b c d e

14   :

a b c d e

15   :

a b c d e

16   :

a b c d e

Section 4 — Analogies

In these questions there are two figures on the left separated by an arrow. You have to decide how these two figures are related. There is a third figure which is separated by an arrow from five further figures on the right. You have to decide which one of these five figures is related to the third figure in the same way as the first two figures are related to each other. Mark your choice on the answer sheet.

Example

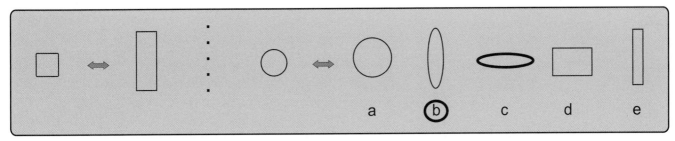

1.

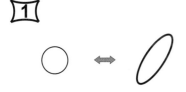 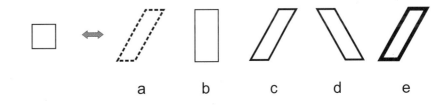

2.

 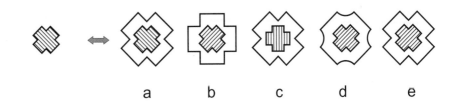

3.

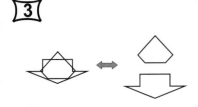 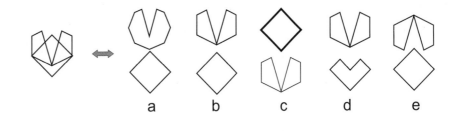

4.

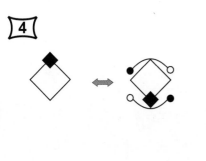 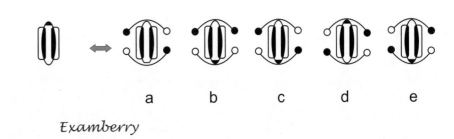

Section 4 Page 2

5

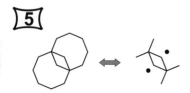 :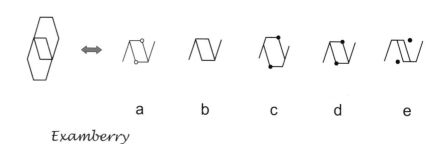

a   b   c   d   e

6

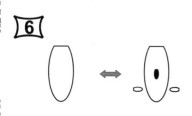 :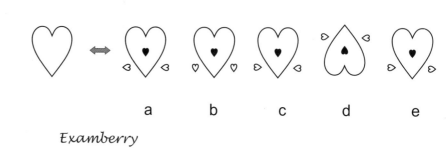

a   b   c   d   e

7

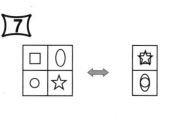 :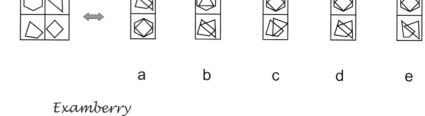

a   b   c   d   e

8

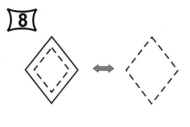 :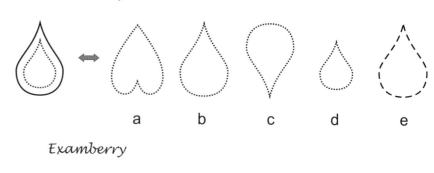

a   b   c   d   e

9

 :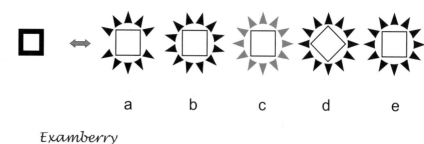

a   b   c   d   e

10

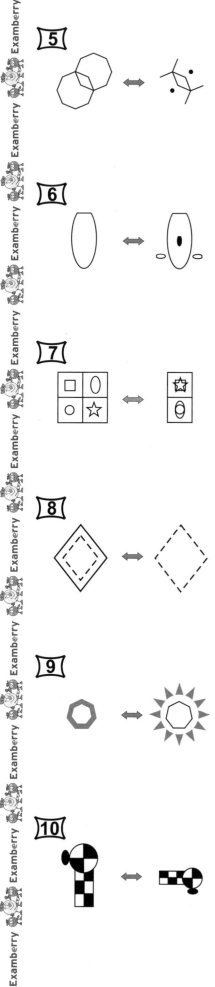 :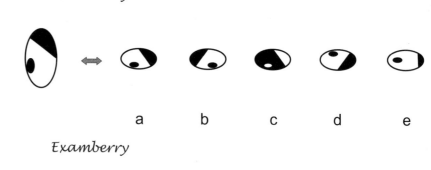

a   b   c   d   e

Section 4 Page 3

[11]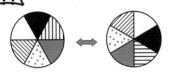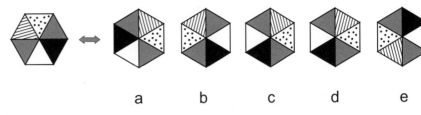

a b c d e

[12]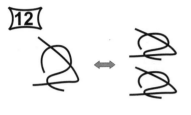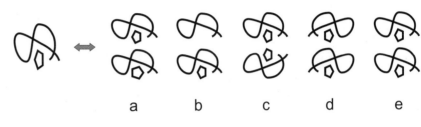

a b c d e

[13]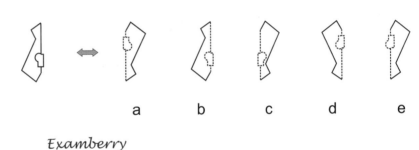

a b c d e

[14]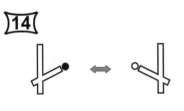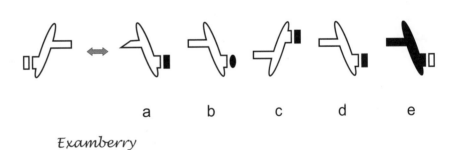

a b c d e

[15]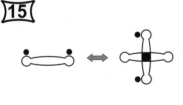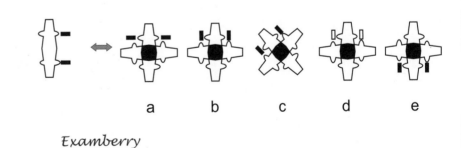

a b c d e

[16]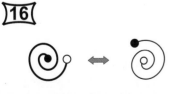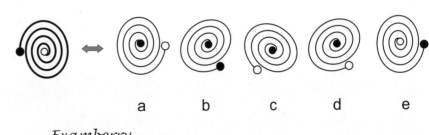

a b c d e

Section 5   Series

In these questions there is a series of five squares on the left. The figures within these squares form a logical sequence but one of the squares has been left blank. You have to decide which one of the five figures on the right should occupy the empty square. Mark your choice on the answer sheet.

Example

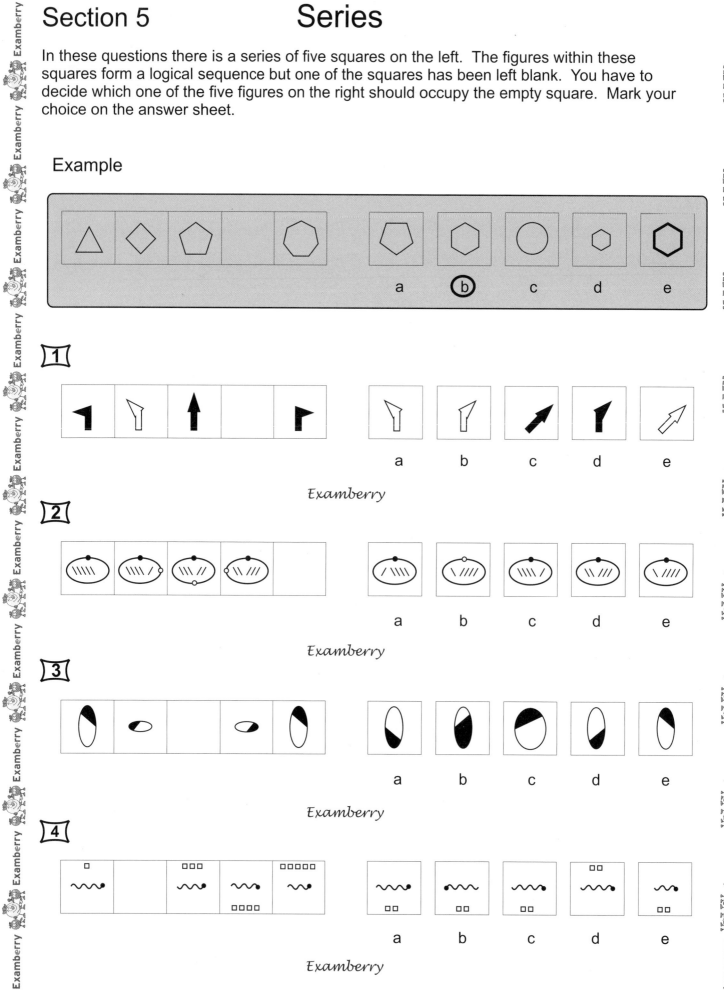

Section 5 Page 2

5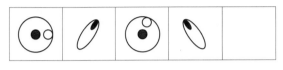

a   b   c   d   e

6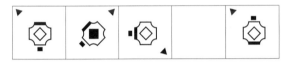

a   b   c   d   e

7

a   b   c   d   e

8

a   b   c   d   e

9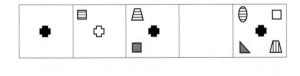

a   b   c   d   e

10

Section 5 Page 3

11

a b c d e

12

a b c d e

13

a b c d e

14

a b c d e

15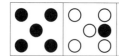

a b c d e

16

a b c d e

End of Test